Looking Askance

Laura Klinkon

Stesichorus Publications

Acknowledgments

"People may look," was performed on March 24, 2013 in the Photoplay Program of the MuCCC Theater in Rochester, N.Y.; "Thence from hence" was written September 7, 2013 from an ekphrastic prompt provided by Just Poets member M.J. Iuppa; "The mail gave me the flu" appeared in the April 2014 issue of *Canto Magazine* online; "Divide the apples" was published in the *2017 Le Mot Juste*; "I liked you better before" was read on February 22, 2015 at the St. John Fisher College Skalny Welcome Center as sponsored by Rochester Poets.

Copyright © 2017 by Laura Klinkon
All rights reserved. No portion of this work may be reproduced or transmitted in any form or by any means, electronic or mechanical, including photocopying and recording, or by any information storage and retrieval system, without written permission from the author.

Cover concept: Laura Klinkon
Design Consultation: Editions Printing

Published by Stesichorus Publications, Rochester, N.Y.

ISBN: 978-0-9986405-1-8
First Edition

Looking Askance

Laura Klinkon

It is difficult not to write satire.
....
Indignation will drive me to verse, such as I—or any scribbler—
May still command. All human endeavors...make
The mixed mash of my verse.

                                              Juvenal, *Satire I*

Contents

Introduction	9
I went to the city today	11
People may look	12
Some tides rise	13
Scattered clouds	15
Thence from hence	16
After the concert	17
Self-possessed	18
Glancing at the pot today	19
The mail gave me the flu	21
She scowls	23
Divide the apples	24
Faux paw	25
Snake desire	26
Today you liked my shirt	27
Parody of an anticipated parody	28
I know your language	29
Wirble	30
The wedding	31
A political soliloquy	32
I liked you better before	33
Looking at a lemon	34
My heart is a pip	35

Introduction

One can write several poems over time, gather them together in ways that seem appropriate, and, even once collected, ask oneself just what kind of poems they are. Though I am fairly certain the poems in *Looking Askance* belong together, I have been hard put to characterize them.

I have thought of these poems as satirical and tried to pinpoint whether they fall under the classical Horatian, Juvenalian, or Menippean categories, that is, light-hearted, critical, or cynical, but none of these labels seem to fit quite. I've also tried to determine whether they are political satire, but political satire, including its classical categories would require a more objective point of view. That is to say, satire should be looking outward and not inward.

In my understanding satire also entails humor, and I believe regarding satirical humor, that it occurs when an observed phenomenon suddenly strikes us as true or commonplace, though we are well aware it is rarely talked about. In this sense, I believe these poems are humorous.

Nevertheless, the objectivity one expects of satirical humor is missing here, for these poems look inwards while only obliquely "looking askance" from a highly personal orientation towards a highly specific interpersonal event.

The result, I would say, is pathetic, because the persona in these poems is distressed—mostly due to a fundamental frustration encountered in communicating with others. Granted that the "look" is at first directed inward, it then turns to group and interpersonal experiences, and then towards annoyingly disinclined personalities, whose reasons for being so are only insinuated.

I conclude that these poems are humorous satire with pathos. But are they political? Insofar as the behavior insinuated reflects current mores, they could be. On the other hand, these poems touch on distressing minutiae only theoretically linked to today's distorted, mediated, and confounding dys-communication.

The Author, Sept. 10, 2017

I went to the city today

I went to the city today where
others awaited not me, but it was
okay, I had little to say, so they
made some space for me.

The talk was of everything not of
the city, but strangers that haunt
contingency realms, their customs
impenetrable, beliefs unshakeable,
we ought to just leave them alone.

When I got home, I looked up
the word 'bone'—it was one thing
I hadn't dared say, or maybe I said it,
'What is your weight in bone?'

I had learned that nearby, many
strangers abide. As I might have done
too, my first thought attending,
but this is the misapplication of will,
you ought not what you want,
but your will, you'll fare better that way.

I went to the city today, without
any thrill into play, yet I let it arise
while I covered my eyes, as my chair
soundly found its own clay. When
passion appears, it may set you arrears,
but today, as it were, I was keenly all ears.
Today, I was keenly all ears.

People may look

Some people may look askance
Some people may look a-sky
Some people will look awry at me
No matter how hard I try!

Some tides rise

My pink shirt on the ironing board,
my empty sandals in sight,
the shorts I couldn't find—
before me,
the key still in the door,
the phone securely
on the hook—
I've been pondering
various projects
incomplete,
each message
I could think of
now
in transit,
measured the hollow
niches
to disinfect
or cover up,
and now I remember
Giacomo da
Lentini's wavering
notion that
low tides
rise
even when there's
no ocean
and all is
locked
inside;
my toes are
nicely
manicured,
my jeans
a little wide,

I used to
do cartwheels
my mother busy
in the next room,
I wonder what
she thought;
old newspapers
in shallow
ditches
need to be
cleaned out and
some tides
rise.

Scattered clouds

The event announcement
says: "scattered clouds"
presumably predicting
the weather during
the show—or does it mean
conditions while deciding?
My clouds are often
scattered—one cloud for who
I hope to see, another for
who I fervidly hope
not to, one for what I think
I'll gain by going, one for in-
convenient questions I may incur, one
for where I'd like to sit
and the time ahead I'd need
to get there—naturally,
what I should wear, and if I
should have had my hair done
in advance, what friend to invite
or not, and then I imagine the various
kinds of greetings and nods
I should bestow or withhold,
then if I'll stay to the end
or leave early, and even whether
I'll need to go at all, having
all sorts of chores to do
at home. All of these clouds do
sometimes gather 'round me, less and less
scattered, more and more threatening
a major storm. I'll surely bring an umbrella,
or pick out a weatherproof cover
...for my bed! I may not even
pick up the phone.

Thence from hence

Do I have miles to go?
Do I need to traipse
through this snow?
Will I wet my toes?

I think there are signposts
bright enough to see, if
there's no more snow
and the fates decree.

There's a fence thence
to be reached from hence;
but will the snow
be dense?

Should I return
whence I came?
Would I put me to shame,
returning hence?

After the concert

I sat as if I understood,
looked...as if I recognized,
obsequiously begged pardon and shrinking
gave way...to intimate propriety.

Correctly used no fingers
for my food, my weaving
through the klatsches ruffled
no one, shillyshallied only
over hanging up my coat.

Fervid ficelles I fluidly flung,
the fringe phalanx finessing,
fine feeling flowing, facetious
fascicles floating, finally fracking
a fearful but friendly facade.

Upon openings pensively promulgated,
pilgrim to pillars of prompt arrivés,
I formed a question about what then
to say, but finding no answer, blurted
my best—a dubious test, kindly taken in jest.

I bid my thread rewind, adjusted my shoe,
my head nearly thumping the banister,
my breath blew a shallow "til I see you,"
and scrabbling my coat, I withdrew.

The glow beginning to dwindle,
outdoors the lights were blue, I saw
all I was, done, knew...could be entwined
in a bundle and trundled as a bien vivante,
bon voyagée courante.

Self-possessed

As I look at all the self-possessed faces
in little squares about a half-inch each
I marvel at how well some are obscured
by photographic camouflage while others
are displayed in what appears as frankness.
Naturally one looks at those a longer time
until we have divined the truth we
think they say: I am as peaceful and collected
as a Renaissance madonna, or as thrilled
with life as any ever was, or as ready to admit
my rank humility, or as righteous and resolved,
as glamorous and sedate, ineffable
as loving, or as primly bored as you are, or as openly
alert, or as seeking new horizons, or convincingly
agnostic, or resignedly industrious, am I sure I got them
all? While others show not faces but some substituting object,
painting, symbol, logo, landscape, borrowed face, to
hide behind. These at first attract attention in the
most dramatic way, but once noted, one just wonders
what deep meaning they betray.... It's a question—
which is better: symbol? landscape? frankly me?
If, let's say, a landscape stops me, I may look a little
more: falling waters, widening vista, swoop and
glide to distant shores.... I'll go too, perhaps with you!
Fine-line drawing, country symbol tell me of your state
and taste, or if funny, somewhat knowing—may cast doubt on
how I rate! I prefer the full-face photos, still and silent as
they seem. You will likely think they're steady...chances are,
they'll always be. Needn't tell what lies uncovered;
ache our gently probing minds—gently too, may be confusing...
better "Like" then out of mind.

Glancing at the pot today

Glancing at the pot today,
I thought I saw it's lips, that is,
the space between the rim and
tam o' shanter lid, moving in a
smile over its stout, placidly
round belly—handles or elbows
poised assuredly—a simple,
but friendly, dependable pal.

How can a hat or lid, cover and smile
simultaneously? A feat of lithe affability
it seems: the brim/rim smiling, the handles—
protective elbows or attentive ears,
the topknot sporting a jaunty humor,
the tummy stowing a sweet amuse-bouche.

Yet such a smile! Perhaps relieved
after I'd shut off the heat? Or honeying
up for a return smile of acknowledgment?
Or gloating over gourmet poires épicées? Or just
trying to appease me when noticing
my impatience that very moment...?

Do pots have a soul? Or
do we transfer ours to them?
If tomorrow, I feel gloomy, will my
pot feel the same? Questions worthy of
Kierkegaard...who might have reflected
on desire, feelings, gourmandise,
empathy.... Why shouldn't the pot
after all, experience satisfaction? And
as in humans, enjoyment cools and the pot
empties.... Existential dread!

A sensitive cook is obliged to smile
encouragement—I believe K. and we
might agree: This IS about relationships.

And this IS a faithful pot. Even
if I should come down with squirrel-
transmitted or aluminum-leached
poisoning, I would persevere with this
steadfast, iron-clad pot, its bonhomie
not to be passed over or easily relinquished
...a question of dependency, admittedly....

Reminding me of my friend who's similar:
stout, solidly round (though squarish),
especially sensitive..., to himself, that is.
My friend...who has not returned my message....
Me, hoping for a smiley response.... Ha!
Could this be the reason I've fixated on
this pot? Could this be about projection?
My impatience with the pears—really my
resentment of my friend's silence. Had I
felt better if the pot had whistled...?

Well, by now the pears are cooler—I can put them
in the freezer—along with my friend
if he hasn't answered soon.

The mail gave me the flu

The mail gave me the flu
or was it the male? Both
could not be right
unless the regular mail—man
is back. The woman could
never have done it...not
as I could tell. "Don't you have
a plowman?" she asked as if I
deserved one from my clearly
well-born looks.... She caught my
irony, too: "Didn't feel like
walking to his house over there."
She grinned...then honked when
turning around...also checking
that I'd be okay.... The man
would've looked, then...shrugged!

Was it someone at the
post-office? Does anthrax
fly again? Right through
my Skype connection all
the way from Leghorn?
Was it my aunt whose
imaginary illnesses infect
even the floor joists? Or
might it have been my
son calling at night from
China making me rush
from my bed to the cold
kitchen to catch the call...
then hanging up? Or did my
other son pick up a bug
in a Caribbean conch?

It's probably my pick
of all these possibilities.
My choice? ...hmm.... Oh,
has my cough cleared already?!

So..., if I could only concentrate on
the conch and not the bug, the
floor instead of the joists,
the next night's call
instead of the rush, on my
flying to Leghorn and not
the anthrax flying here,
the complicit honk and not
the shrug..., the chivalry of hope
and not the flu.

She scowls

She scowls...
she almost growls!
What next will pass her jowl?
Will she howl?

Don't the least know why!
Must I cry? fly? decry?
Is she odd, cruel, or sly?
I am sorely tried....

Her inverted smile
infers perverse guile;
to protest at trial?
What complaint to file?

Yet she's reached an age
past her prime, I'd gauge;
she'd appear a sage
if she'd curb her rage.

Devotees she keeps
and they bow quite deep,
yet I think they weep
when her ire they reap.

In homage—she craves,
all may crouch as knaves
or as slaves behave when
her switch she waves.

No, I'd not devined
she was so inclined;
friendship's hard to find
in a brow so lined.

Loosen up, my girl!
Let joy shout, unfurl!
Your resentment hurl—
like your cat its burls.

Divide the apples

Separate the apples,
smaller from the larger,
pock-marked from the clear;
no, don't set them in one basket—
ensure they're dry, and
place them so they'll breathe.

Small green apples one a day
they say can keep you healthy
like a good, reliable friend;
the larger, bombastic, prone to
tragic blemishes, may need to be
put by quickly, or let go..., even
before you dare begin to peel.

Faux paw

My, what a mutt I am!
My soul is just not waggish enough
to prowl with the utmost pedi-
greed, refined—those who won't
be fined, of course, even if they
themselves connive a faux paw;
such contrivances may be revered,
and some much prized, for subtle
poignancy or clearly superior mirth.

Ah, you're waiting for the howler. So!
Absently scouring for something to do,
like Lassie (yes, I watch those old
reruns), I rustled up a job a chum
was just not doing..., tapping into
help from another chum (hers!)—whence
he declared the work too easy and not
the least indispensable. 'What did I want?'
they growled, I ambling away disheartened.
I might have yowled, 'A cool drink, please,
with a splash of sweet kennel-aderie.'

But, who was I to be volunteering?
So much for jobs mutts mustn't do.
To think I might have slurped their
gourmet chow with rabid satisfaction!

The moral: with job-eat-job, only bones to gnaw
or pick or chew come paw-in-paw for mutts.

Snake desire

heavy rains, late-hour waking
mufffled shrugs doff boa clouds
...my Skype's half-hearted ring

speech cut through by shrieking sirens
profiles, lips constricted, turn away...light-
crazed panes, steely retorts to vacant skies

impetuous offers, off-hand salutations,
automatic rendezvous. Why or Why bother
zings through tendons, snaking desires.

Today you liked my shirt

Today you liked my shirt.
You know, I bought it 20 years
ago and there's a hole right
in front I was going to
patch with a flower cut
from the shoulder pad.

You didn't notice these
colors, exciting as they
seem, are not inborn in me:
climbing fandango roses
trellised on viridian and black...
alluring, likely suited
to one of yours.

It has appeal for just those
traits that don't belong to me:
youthful, sanguine, sweet, enticing.
On zesty days...a trace perhaps.
But today, an odysseic tragedy:
solitude...of the deepest kind.

I approach you in self-disdain;
your racy sirens tear at
my advantages, laugh at my
singularity, document my diffidence.
What remains as a response?

This shirt—a shroud hung
on the bones of a mazurka-stepping
apparition, sings romance with
not a shred of hope. Yes, one could say
"shroud shirt".... Don't you see?
It's already been chewed.

Parody* of an anticipated parody

A book of Prized Philosophies bedecks my étagère
my Sophist thongs stand by prepared and
bloomers from Found Objects
dry in the shower
the door coquettishly ajar;
my e-mail enticements
modestly extended,
I've measured
the fenceless
areas in my royaume
to drive with pikes
or strew with rosy hand
grenades
and wistfully I remember
my own or someone else's
original notion
that each work by every bosun
arises from
Universal Ocean
which boatworthy friends
with glee are free
to find and treasure
as chance may guarantee.
My nails are
sweetly
sharpened
my sharkskin coat
is sleeked
I used to do nosedives
at the piscine
to drain away the neighbors—
they never had a clue;
glistening creations sighted
in stirring waters
need to be hauled in—should gems
with flotsam
flow.

*See "Some tides rise," p. 13

I know your language

I know your language
but I don't like you—
cautiously smiling,
sensing part of me isn't
agreeable. Well, it's
head to head with impressions
we have built: me, I'm lazy,
lacking clarity; you, intolerably
sharp and busy, sometimes as a
busybody blasting me
for taking all things slowly;
What am I waiting for? you ask.
There's not so much to pe-
netrate! Why bother when a
twinkly sunshine sham
of neighbor love is all that is
required to keep aloft mirages
of affection. Side by side,
occasionally as needed we will
soon enough discover who we are
and then commit to liking us forever—
ugh, never, says my sloth-like pacing.
It's all about beliefs and habits:
What are yours? It's all about de-
ciding if you trust enough to tell
the truth; I know I tell the truth
too much, perhaps.... Who needs it?
Let us smile at god's creation and the
crazy odds we share dividers in this
holy hell hotel. We needn't plumb the depths,
only measure how we split the power—no,
not the heat—it's always
summer here, or spring at least,
and if the kitchen smells don't mingle
well, we'll just turn up our fans. It's
possible to do—without regret.
Why go beyond our fine devices for
decorum and good cheer? It's okay,
I think, to share one beer.

Wirble

Making salad out of boredom—
am remembering how she said I
should toss vinegar and honey,
though it seemed the dousing should
have come from me. Didn't outright say
what I silently was sure of, trusting that the pieces
would be settling into place themselves.

So, the honey I accepted,
though the vinegar was dubious, for it
soothed away the sour that was burbling
in my veins; yes, it smoothed away the sour
that was wirbling in my brain.

The wedding

I went to a wedding
the bridesmaids in black
the sermon begged mercy
from powers above,
prayed all be inviolate from
hardness of heart;
close kinsmen upholding the
tempering of pride,
the priest then
remembering
the solace bequeathed us through
sufferings of Christ,
love steadfast enduring
God's glory extolling;
so pledging allegiance
to church and to peace
the humble pair fumble
the gold ring retrieving, yet
patient they beam
at the party's good cheer
the holy man's blessing,
praise be for the Mrs. and
Perfect Companion—he
fervent caducean, she a
nice girl he'd known.

A political soliloquy

Look at my face.
It's like a polished apple;
people have been polishing
and cleaning me up now
for decades—in fact, I've taken
a shine to this apple myself...
and, while not a teacher,
I trust I'm a credible model;
no worm in this apple—
technology, sociology, the media,
and the Middle Class, have
oblterated my annelid;

I'm specially popular with fems, ya know,
but haven't quite gone viral;
a polished apple, even without worms,
mind you, has always been suspect. Think
how often Eve had to spit on hers before
taking the bite! Some still ask if it was mere
persistent vanity that burnished this mother
of all Malus Domesticus. Look at the eyes
in this apple please.... Surgically stitched,
though the right keeps tending to wink.

One may wonder what lies within my
extirpated worm hole.... Let me just say this:
it's lined with jewels. In fact, when they
make my death mask, it will be replicated
large and small and many times in gold.
If I were you, I'd bid for a hat pin or even
a mantel piece.

I liked you better before

I liked you better before you had your
colonoscopy. You must have felt like
a new man, after the techy had clipped
and swept away your polyps, like
getting a haircut or having stiff ends
shorn from your ears. At last
you could wear your Bavarian Alpine
with bristly brush in proper fit, and
finally your ear phones wouldn't be a joke
while jogging. (I always have wondered
whether your run really kept time with
your beat.) It must have felt good
being in the race again—I mean,
after your colo-rectal.

Still, I detected a shudder and a gulp
when you told us, as if your
rectum had been suddenly whammed
against the wall of an arctic cave
reminding you the polar tour
was slightly on the upscale side.
Amazing, since you usually try not to
divulge your secrets, fears, or feelings—
whenever you may have them. Yet after a while,
your reticence turned further inward—
hermetic with a definitely decorous flare,
subtly tinged with smug. No, no, not smut—
that had already been taken care of!
When your cataracts were removed, you
almost invited empathy, the lens somewhat
wobbling in your freshly swollen orbs.
You felt stinging, you confessed, and I was oh
so privileged to commiserate. Was it this event
entrenched your motto: Inspire no pity?

Lens have since firmed and orbs retracted;
a telling eye has examined your entrails.
In the meantime, on my side, we have acquired
a white Mercedes. Won't it be great to have to
brush off the smut only once in a while?

Looking at a lemon

I'm looking at a lemon—the part
that's had the stem plucked off—lop-
sided, precariously turned towards me: a
botoxed eye...a pursed, pinched lip...a
belly-button? Or just an elliptical shape
askew.... Or...a recently hatched chick or,
a brassy cocked behind?

It makes me think you should have been a blond,
I mean, how could you not have been a blond? Your
twin made off with your birth scalp, right? So sad...hmmm. I'm
not feeling happy with you today.... Can you tell?

Judging from that wrinkled rind, neither are you with me. How
can you peer so one-eyed blank? Don't you know I've
been upset with you? Are you just too yellow
to discuss it? Do you use your mouth only
to sour me with people I LOVE? I'm sure
you have enough acidity to go around.... Or are you
soured? Is it something I did you're not prepared
to call me on?

Surely you know I wouldn't do the same to you.
To people important to me, I always explain.
Of course you know..., but no way
will you loose that lip. Tell me,
do you think it's smarter that way? Or just long-term
more convenient for you to simply
cock your butt?

What should I do? The same to you? Well,
keep staring me down and you will see,
after I dice you up and squeeze you dry,
what's coming to you!

My heart is a pip

My heart is a pip*
poison as an apple seed
slippery as a lemon's
crimped in a leather rind
cracked from the inside
cast and spotted like a die
epaulette for a scrubbed cadet
won by a card toss
diseased by contagion
drooping like a May lily
set off by squeaky sounds

*(See *The Free Dictionary* by Farlex)

About the author

Laura Klinkon, née DiLiberto in the Province of Enna, Sicily, grew up in Pittsburgh, Pa., studied literature and language at the University of Pittsburgh and at American University in Washington, D.C., completing additional coursework at various other universities, including New York University, Middlebury College, and the Rochester Institute of Technology. She has been employed in teaching, editing, free-lance writing, and translating in various cities including New York, Washington, D.C., and her adopted home town of Rochester, N.Y., where she has also raised two children together with her former husband, Heinrich Klinkon, now deceased. She has been a member of Just Poets and Rochester Poets as well as a member of Writers & Books in Rochester, N.Y.; she has read her poems in the Eastman School of Music *Women in Music* Festival, and appeared in several anthologies, including *Liberty's Vigil* and the Just Poets annual *Le Mot Juste*, as well as consecutively in the monthly online *Canto Magazine*. She has read in the Genessee Reading Series of Writers & Books and in a *Poetry as Philosophy* series with poet and philosopher David White, at Books, Etc. in Macedon, N.Y. and at the St. John Fisher College Skalny Center sponsored by Rochester Poets. In 2013 she published her full-length book of poems *Trying to Find You* with Kernel-Image, and in 2017, the chapbooks *Kitchen Abrasives* and *Looking Askance*, under the Stesichorus Publications, Rochester, N.Y. imprint.